BEES

BEES

TOM JACKSON

This pocket edition first published in 2024

First published in a hardback edition in 2021

Copyright © 2024 Amber Books Ltd

Published by
Amber Books Ltd
United House
London N7 9DP
United Kingdom

www.amberbooks.co.uk
Instagram: amberbooksltd
Pinterest: amberbooksltd
Twitter: @amberbooks

ISBN: 978-1-83886-357-9

Project Editor: Anna Brownbridge
Designer: Keren Harragan and Andrew Easton
Picture Research: Terry Forshaw

Printed in China

Contents

Introduction

Never underestimate a bee. These unassuming insects go about their busy days, filling sunny flower beds and meadows with their tranquil, whirring buzz. Perhaps, upon seeing them, our first and only thought is, 'Oh good, it's not a wasp.' A bee is indeed less likely to wield its stinger, not least because honeybees are doomed to die should they use this ultimate weapon. What we forget to consider is that working largely unseen, the bees are an incredibly productive group. Of course, honeybees are the first to spring to mind, workaholic insects that create complex societies for producing honey, one of the most valued of all

foodstuffs. But, additionally, there is an impressive array of bees that live in other ways: mason bees build homes out of mud, while orchid bees collect exotic oils to woo suitors. And all this is powered only by foods made from pollen and nectar.

The world of bees will surely surprise and amaze, but we also need the hidden power of bees to pollinate and propagate our crops. We ignore threats to the world's bees at our peril.

ABOVE:
A Cape honeybee on a red aloe plant
in southern Africa.

OPPOSITE:
Honeybees at a hive are a close-knit, hard-working
team focused on producing honey for their young –
and for human consumption.

Social Bees

Bees are famous for being sociable, living together in colonies or hives that contain hundreds or perhaps many thousands of individual bees. All the bees are working together for the common good under the rule of a single, all-powerful queen. The most familiar social bees are honeybees, but bumblebees and stingless bees also live this communal life. Nevertheless, the social bee species constitute a small fraction – less than 1,000 species out of more than 20,000 – of the broader bee group, Anthophila. The bee's gregarious way of life, which is shared with their more beastly cousins, such as yellow-jacket wasps and ants, is the most extreme form of social group seen in the animal kingdom. The queen is the only reproductive female, and the rest of the colony are her infertile daughters. These females work to raise their sisters to swell the ranks of workers, and on occasion a few brothers, too. The system works well because of a genetic quirk in the way a bee's sex is determined. It is normal for offspring and siblings to share half their genes, and this level of relatedness is enough for them to be altruistic toward each other, up to a point. However, male social bees have half the number of genes as females, and this skews genetic relatedness. Worker bees share three-quarters of their genes with their sisters, which includes the next generation of queens. This stronger genetic link is enough for a female to abandon her own breeding opportunity and work to boost that of her sisters.

OPPOSITE:

Spot the queen

The queen – shown here in a domestic hive in Italy by the spot of green paint – is considerably larger than her workers. The size difference is due to enlarged ovaries for producing fertile eggs.

OVERLEAF:

Carniolan honeybee

Named after the coastal region of Slovenia, the Carniolan honeybee is the main kind of honeybee in the Balkans and northern Italy, where there is a tradition of giving hives a brightly painted pattern. This subspecies of the western honeybee, nicknamed 'carnies', is known worldwide for producing healthy hives, resistant to pests.

ABOVE:

Honeycomb

All honeybees build a nest comprised of hexagonal cells. This is the near optimal compromise between the nest having high rigidity as well as maximizing the volume.

RIGHT:

Cape honeybee

The Cape bee is a subspecies of *Apis mellifera*, the western honey bee. It clings to the very tip of southern Africa around the Western Cape region, where it is a crucial pollinator in local agriculture and natural habitats. This forager is gathering pollen from an evergreen shrub called orange jasmine.

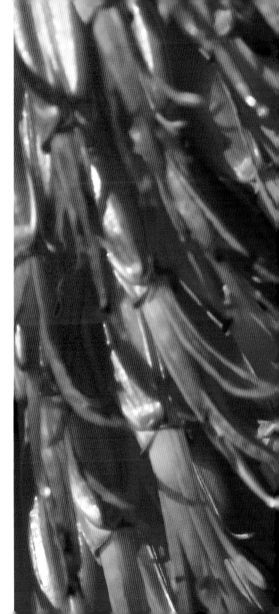

Sneaky breeder

A Cape honeybee collects nectar from a Cape aloe. Cape honeybees are unique among the western honeybees in that the female workers – or at least a few of them – can lay fertile diploid eggs. Diploid eggs have a double set of genes and so develop into females – effectively the cloned daughters of the 'laying worker'. In areas where the Cape honeybee lives alongside other subspecies, the laying workers can sneak eggs into neighbouring nests where they are raised by the unsuspecting – and unrelated – worker bees.

Caucasian honeybee
Named for the Caucasus Mountains, this subspecies, *Apis mellifera caucasia*, is also common in Turkey and the northern parts of the Middle East. They do not do well in colder climates, and are not well suited to beekeeping because they are most active at the end of summer, whereas most nectar sources become abundant in spring.

OPPOSITE:
Cretan honeybee
A worker bee of the subspecies endemic to Crete is gathering nectar to take back to the hive. This subspecies, *Apis mellifera adami*, was only identified in 1975, and has a varied genetic profile. This suggests it is actually a hybridization of Mediterranean strains that has developed on the Greek island due to beekeepers bringing in new varieties of bee.

Giant honeybee

This species, *Apis dorsata*, lives across southeast Asia from the foothills of the Himalayas to the Wallace Line, which divides Asian wildlife from Australasian fauna. At about 17–20mm (0.7–0.8in) long, the giant name is apt, it being 70 percent bigger than most other honey bees.

OPPOSITE:

A queen and her court

A western honeybee
queen is surrounded by
her court, laying eggs
into the 'broodcomb'
– the part of the wider
honeycomb set aside for
raising young.

ABOVE:

Drinking up

As their name suggests,
honeybees eat mostly
honey, and exclusively for
those bees confined to
the hive. However, these
foraging workers are
pausing mid-flight to lap
up a drink of water with
their feathery, tongue-
like mouthparts.

Eastern honeybee
The species *Apis cerana*
is native to South and
East Asia. Only the
Indian subspecies has
been domesticated for
honey production. The
eastern species is very
similar to the western
honeybee, *A. mellifera*,
in size but has discernibly
thinner yellow stripes.

OVERLEAF:
Black dwarf honeybee
A close-up of the head
and mouthparts of the
black dwarf honeybee,
Apis andreniformis,
shows the feathery
tongue-like mouthpart
called the glossum.
This is used to slurp
up liquids – nectar,
honeydew, water, and,
of course, honey.
A. andreniformis lives in
the forests of Southeast
Asia. It is about 6.5mm
(0.25in) long, about
half the length of a
domestic honeybee.

LEFT:

Swarm

A giant honeybee swarm hangs from a tree branch. This wild swarm will have recently split from a parent colony that was growing too large. A new queen is protected at the centre.

ABOVE:

Domestic animal

Workers busy themselves at the entrance to a domestic hive in Italy. Honeybees have been domesticated for at least 4,500 years, probably first in ancient Egypt. Our ancient ancestors collected honey from wild nests.

OVERLEAF LEFT:

African honeybee

A swarm of *Apis mellifera scutellata* gathers on a pipe. It is likely that the subspecies is an ancestral form of the western honeybee species, which spread out from East Africa about 7 or 8 million years ago.

Dwarf bee

A red dwarf honeybee, *Apis florea*, laps a drop of water on the lip of a sink. This species broadly overlaps with that of its similarly diminutive close relative, the black dwarf honeybee, in Southeast Asia. However, the red species is also found in much of the Indian subcontinent and even parts of the Middle East that have rainfall high enough for forests to grow.

OPPOSITE:

Wild hive

A nest of red dwarf honeybees is teeming with bodies. This species migrates and swarms regularly, driven by its dry habitats to find new places to set up a nest and forage.

ABOVE:

Maltese honeybee

The dark subspecies *Apis mellifera ruttneri*, is native to Malta, and is known for being more aggressive than most honeybees, often attacking animals that stray close to the nests.

Cyprus honeybee
This subspecies, *Apis mellifera cypria*, is native to the island of Cyprus in the Eastern Mediterranean. It is a sedate bee that tends not to swarm, even when the hot summer temperatures reduce the supply of flowers.

ABOVE:
Unique defence
Recent research has found that Cyprus honeybees kill
invading predators, such as hornets, by smothering
them in a ball of bodies until the attacker asphyxiates.
Other subspecies use the balling technique to kill by
overheating the enemy.

Bumblebee
Chunky bumblebees are
another kind of social
bee. They live in much
smaller colonies, with a
queen bumblebee ruling
over 50 to 100 daughters.

**Bumblebee versus
honeybee**
There are many more
types of bumblebee than
honeybee. The former
group has 250 members
to the seven species
of honeybee.

White-tailed bumblebee
Most bumblebees belong
to the *Bombus* genus.
This one is *B. magnus*,
or the northern white-
tailed bumblebee, which
is seen across Europe,
especially in open
moorland habitats.

Plant foods

As with other social bees, the bumblebees consume nectar and pollen, with foragers carrying it back to the nest to share with the workers and to feed to brooding larvae. However, unlike honeybees and stingless bees, the insects do not produce honey in the true sense. They provision their young with small amounts of regurgitated nectar and chewed pollen, which forms a sweet paste.

What's the buzz?

The name bumblebee
is said to have emerged
from the low, persistent
buzz these insects make
in flight, plus their oddly
slow and ponderous
demeanour, as if they are
bumbling from flower
to flower. At least, that
is one of a few theories
behind their distinctive
name.

LEFT:

Eyes not ears

Bumblebees cannot hear – they have no ears – but can probably detect vibrations through other body parts. The eyes and antennae, which detect chemicals, are the primary sense organs.

ABOVE:

Flight system

Bumblebees beat their wings 200 times a second. Each beat is not controlled by a single nerve signal – that would be too slow a command system. Instead the flight muscles vibrate like a taut string and this creates the high frequency of beats.

LEFT:
Warming up
Bumblebees appear earlier in the spring than honeybees and thrive in colder locales. This is due in part to the insulation afforded by their thick 'fur' coats. However, the cold-blooded insects also warm themselves up by absorbing the sun's heat with their dark bodies and by shivering the flight muscles to generate some internal warmth.

OVERLEAF:
Pollinators
As with all social bees and many other flying insects, bumblebees are important pollinators, ensuring that plants are able to transfer pollen needed to breed and develop seeds. Flowers produce nectar to attract the bees and, in return, the bees transport sticky pollen grains on their bristled bodies – unwittingly – from flower to flower.

Old and new worlds

The tree bumblebee, or *Bombus hypnorum*, lives in Europe and northern Asia, spreading all the way to the Pacific coast of Siberia. Bumblebee species also live in North and South America, plus the northern fringe of Africa. However, they are not found south of the Sahara or in Australia.

Stingless bees

Most social bees are so-called stingless bees. These insects actually do have stingers but they are so small as to be useless. The stingless bees, of which there are about 500 species, often have a more waspish look, with a narrow 'waist' between thorax and abdomen.

Brood parasite

Like its avian namesake, the lemon cuckoo bumblebee, *Bombus citrinus*, from the northeast of North America, does not raise its own young. Instead it sneaks eggs into the brood chambers of other species of bumblebee and fools their workers into doing it for them. This mode of reproduction is called brood parasitism.

Bite not sting
A squad of older members from a stingless bee colony in Brazil (the species is *Scaptotrigona xanthotricha*) are seconded as soldiers and rush to the broad entrance of the nest. Without a sting the bees will bite, and some species have a nasty acidic saliva that aggravates the wound.

ABOVE:
Nests
Stingless bees make their nests in cavities in rotting
wood, dead trees and underground. The nests
generally have a single entrance – and exit – point that
is built to allow a large number of the colony to leave
at the same time.

RIGHT:
Resinous
A *Trigona* stingless bee from Brazil busies herself with
nest maintenance. She is using a paste made from resins
collected from nearby plants to construct the nest.

Beekeeping

Stingless bees have been semi-domesticated in Australia and South and Central America, most notably by the ancient Maya of Mexico and Guatemala. An established colony was collected from the wild by these beekeepers. They looked for nests in logs that could be carried and kept near to their homes.

Fake signal
This Asian species
of stingless bee is
mimicking the warning
colours of wasps and
honeybees to fool
predators into thinking
it carries a stinger.

OPPOSITE:
Stingless bees
Stingless bees are most
abundant in South
America. However, they
are also represented
in Africa, Asia and
Australia. The honey
from this Asian species,
Heterotrigona itama,
is being trialled as a
possible anti-obesity
food supplement.

OVERLEAF:
Bearding
A gang of honeybees
hang out away from the
colony. This activity
is known as bearding
– mostly with a larger
group than this that
looks like a beard (and
is sometimes worn
as one by showmen
and daredevils). The
behaviour occurs before
a swarm or also when the
internal temperature
of the hive is too high.

Solitary Bees

Despite what you may have heard, it is not normal for a bee to live in a large group. Most species – many thousands of types found worldwide in the Anthophila group – are solitary creatures that keep themselves to themselves. As with honeybees and bumblebees, these insects get busy collecting pollen and nectar, but each female builds her own nest and prepares it for her own eggs. How they do this varies from group to group and, as we'll see, the bees use a range of ingenious techniques. Generally this hard work is done during the spring and summer. This sets the stage for eggs to hatch during the autumn, and the larvae – the maggot-like young forms – spend the winter eating their way through a food cache. This is a big ball of pollen and regurgitated nectar that dwarfs the newly-hatched young one. As the weather warms, the now chubby larva will pupate and is soon ready to emerge as an adult.

The males generally emerge first and are just as busy as the females, but less productive. They tend to be smaller than the females due to the shorter development time, but they also need to build a nest or work to provide food for the young. Instead they are simply on the lookout for a mate, which they do by hovering near a nest-building site, or displaying on a perch, advertising their status using a distinctive set of odours.

Solitary bees are not always alone. Some species live in communal settings, with females helping each other out, a hint perhaps of how social bees first appeared.

OPPOSITE:
Orchid bees
Metallic-green orchid bees are so named because they are the sole pollinators of some orchid flowers, although they do visit other kinds of blooms to harvest a nectar with a long proboscis.

Scent collectors
Male orchid bees have comb-like brushes on their legs, which they use to trap the unique fragrances of orchids, other flowers and even rotting wood. This behaviour gives the male bee a distinctive odour, which attracts females during the breeding season.

OPPOSITE:

Carpenter bee

A Caucasian carpenter bee, or *Xylocopa valga*, crawls from its nest in a dead log. These solitary bees are named for the way they cut a nest into wood. There are about 400 species found worldwide. The generic name *Xylocopa* means 'wood cutter'.

ABOVE:

Big and shiny

A violet carpenter bee, *Xylocopa violacea*, seen across Europe and Asia, collects pollen and nectar from a flower. The bee's size – about 25mm (1in) – and vociferous buzz means the insect is superficially mistaken for a bumblebee, but can be told apart by their metallic-looking bodies.

Southern carpenter bee
This view from the top of the head of a male *Xylocopa micans* from the American Deep South and Central America shows the bee's ocelli, or simple eyes, which detect light and dark above – perhaps the shadow of a predator, such as a woodpecker. We know it is a male because of its yellow fluffy hairs. His large compound eyes – bigger than a female's— are used to scan for potential mates.

OPPOSITE:
Home sweet home
Carpenter bees spend the winter – mostly in the larval stage – in a nest dug into wood, such as the branch of this acacia tree. Both males and females spend most of the summer outside searching for mates and collecting food for brooding young.

ABOVE:
Scraping and gouging
Carpenter bees will recycle old nests wherever possible, but if none are available, a female will dig a new one, using her mandibles to cut through the wood. Males do not dig nests.

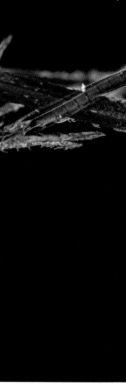

ABOVE:
Resting

A male cuckoo bee clings to the anther of a flower with its legs tucked up. This is called sleeping position, although the sleep in bees is nothing like we experience.

RIGHT TOP:
Neon cuckoo bee

This species, *Thyreus nitidulus*, is from Australia. As a general rule, cuckoo bees parasitize species that look similar to them so they can pass undetected among them.

RIGHT BOTTOM:
Cuckoo bee

These waspish-looking bees do not raise their own young. Instead they are kleptoparasites like their avian namesakes, sneaking into nests and laying an egg in brood cells alongside the host's. Once hatched, the larva cuckoo bee kills their nursery mate – and may eat it – and is thus raised by the stolen labours of an unsuspecting host.

Big mouth
This is a member of the *Nomada* genus, the largest group of cuckoo bees, and with 850 species one of the largest genus of any bee type. As this posture shows, the mandibles of cuckoo bees are especially strong. The larval form has fearsome mouthparts that are the weapons used to kill host larvae in the first moments of life. After developing into an adult, the mandibles are more petite (but not lacking in power) and are devoted to eating pollen and nectar.

OPPOSITE:
Digger bee
As the name suggests, these bees build burrows in the dry earth as shelters and to construct waterproof brood pots for their young. This female *Melissodes* species is collecting pollen from a prickly pear as food for herself and for provisioning her eggs.

ABOVE:
Digger bee
Most of the digger bees belong to the Anthophorini tribe, which is a worldwide group containing about 750 species. However, the digging behaviour is also seen in more distantly related groups, such as the Centridini, which are distinct for collecting oils from flowers instead of pollen.

OVERLEAF:
Urbane digger
The urbane digger bee, *Anthophora urbana*, lives in the United States and Mexico, and is especially common in alpine meadows. This is a male bee as indicated by his white 'bearded' face.

Leafcutter

A female leafcutter bee
hauls a sheet of leaf
cut from a nearby plant
back to her nesting site.
She has chosen a hollow
stick in which to build
the nest and will roll
this and subsequent
leaf fragments into a
compartmentalized tube,
subdivided into brood
chambers for her larvae.

Pugnacious leafcutter bee
This North American species, *Megachile pugnata*, is
a common visitor to sunflowers and related plants. It
is collecting pollen and nectar from a thistle flower.
It will use this food to provision brood chambers back
at the nest.

ABOVE TOP:
Leafcutter bees
A leafcutter bee sleeps on a grass flower. There are around 1,500 species of leafcutter bee, mostly in the *Megachile* genus, and found worldwide. This group includes *M. pluto*, Wallace's giant bee, the largest bee of any kind.

ABOVE BOTTOM:
Chew and slice
Leafcutter bees use their mandibles to slice their way through leaves and sometimes petals to create a very roughly rectangular piece, a bit longer than it is wide, that can be rolled up back at the nest site.

Blue orchard bee
A pair of blue orchard bees, *Osmia lignaria*, prepare to land on a pollen-rich flower. The females build a nest in natural crevices or hollows, near to a supply of soft mud, which is used to line the nest.

Mason bee
As with all bees, mason bees are crucial pollinators, spreading pollen from bloom to bloom. Some North American species, including the orchard bees, are bred specifically to help pollinate commercial crops.

Northerners

Often a mason bee will occupy
the nest hole made by a carpenter bee. There are
about 350 species of mason bee living in the Americas
and across Eurasia. Most of them are found in the
Northern Hemisphere. They are close relatives of the
leafcutter bees and carder bees, which chew up leaves
into a pulp for living nests, and resin bees, which
collect the sticky secretions of trees for that purpose.

LEFT:
Smaller sex

Mining bees are small, ranging from 8–15mm (0.3–0.6in) in length. Male mining bees are smaller and more slender than the females. The males, such as this one catching a bite to eat on a zinnia flower, are not required to do any physical labour building and provisioning of the nests. Mining bees can be distinguished from other kinds by the short velvety tuft of hairs between the eyes.

ABOVE:
In a hole

Mining bees dig communal nests into soft soils, where several females will share the work. The spoil of loose soil creates a chimney around the entrance. There are 1,300 species of mining bees, mostly in the *Andrena* genus, which are found worldwide, except South America and Australasia.

Summer exit
After spending winter in their sealed-off, subterranean brood cells, the newly pupated adults dig themselves out once the temperature above ground reaches about 20°C (68°F).

ABOVE:
Spring mining bee
The *Colletes cunicularius*, the spring mining or vernal
bee, is one of the most widespread of bee species. It
is found in sandy habitats from the British Isles to the
Pacific coast of Siberia. Members of the Colletidae
family are found worldwide but are most abundant
in South America and Australia.

RIGHT:
Late arrival
This large Colletes species – large being over 10mm
(0.4in) – emerges from its underground nest in late
summer. They are active until the end of autumn, by
which time they will have provisioned their eggs
in nests built in loose soils.

Sweat bees

Members of the *Halictidae* family are known as sweat bees. This is because some of them, especially the smaller species, are attracted to sweat. This species is more active at dusk or dawn, using their large ocelli, seen here as dark, shiny spots on the head. The ocelli are simple eyes that help the bees orientate themselves in lower light levels.

Pollen fan
Pollen and nectar are the only source of food for
the sweat bees, or *Halictidae*, and the females
collect it to provide a food store for larvae. The
eggs are laid in underground nests.

OPPOSITE:
Big family
The sweat bee family comprises more than 3,100
species, making it the second largest bee family.
Most species are small for bees, measuring
between 6 and 8mm (0.24 and 0.31in).

Social animals

Most sweat bee species live solitary lives, although they may gather in large groups when the conditions allow. However, some species exhibit eusocial behaviours, similar to those of honeybees, with a queen and workers. Some of these species can only live in this way; others adopt this social system when the supply of food and water make it the best option.

Bee Anatomy

Bees have a highly distinctive body plan, with a set of sleek wings, a lithe but sturdy body, often highlighted with thick pale stripes, a narrow 'waist' mid-body, and a big, busy head. The bee shares these characteristics with a wider group of related insects called the Hymenoptera. This order also contains ants, wasps and sawflies, which outnumber bees ten to one.

The name Hymenoptera could mean 'membrane wing', accounting for the near-transparent wings. However, a better translation is 'married wings', evoking Hymen, the Greek god of marriage. All members of the group have four wings, one large pair in front of a smaller set behind. Each hindwing is attached by hooks to its forewing partner, creating a structure that works as a single flight surface. Additionally, the bees share their tight 'waist' feature with their cousins. In fact, this is much more pronounced in ants and wasps.

Bee anatomy, especially such fine details as the segmentation of the face and abdomen, shows that the bees belong to a single distinct branch of the Apocrita suborder. This group includes ants and wasps and makes up the great majority of the Hymenopterans. Only the sawflies are left out. It seems logical that bees are a closer relative to their more devilish cousins, the yellowjacket wasps – after all, they are of similar stature, both sting and live in colonies of comparable size. However, genetic evidence points to bees being more related to ants.

OPPOSITE:
In sections
As with all insects, a bee's body is organized into three main sections: the head, thorax and abdomen. The head hold the mouthparts and sense organs. The wings and legs are on the thorax, while the abdomen holds most of the internal organs.

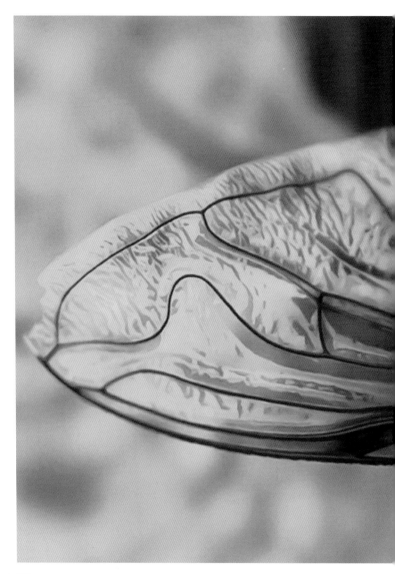

Distinctive vein
Bee wings have a distinctively sturdy vein along the leading edge, seen here at the bottom. This part cuts through the air as the wing flaps up to 200 times per second. It also has a graceful curved shape, while other hymenopterans have more elongated wings.

ABOVE:
Legs on show
Bees have six legs, as do all insects. All three pairs are attached to the midbody thorax section, and they are made up of several jointed sections. The muscles that move the legs – and other body parts – are anchored to the inside of the exoskeleton.

RIGHT:
Mouthparts
Bees have a surprisingly uniform set of mouthparts. The most significant are those that protrude into a flower to slurp up nectar and handle pollen. They include an outer pairing of maxillae, and inner set of two labial palps, and a central tongue-like glossa that is covered in feathery bristles.

Elbows on the head

As this head-on view of a large, parasitic orchid bee, *Exaerte smaragdina*, shows, the antennae (or feelers) of all bees are elbowed, or have a joint half way along.

Segmented feelers
Bee antennae are segmented beyond the elbow. A male bee has 13 segments, while the female always has 12.

LEFT:
Vision

Bees do not see the world in the same way as us. Their large compound eyes are made up of thousands of individual tube-like lenses called ommatidia. These each send an image signal to the animal's brain, which is used to build up a single picture.

ABOVE:
Structural colour

The iridescent colouring of many bees' wings and bodies is not due to chemical pigments. Instead, the rainbow, oil-pattern effect is produced by the way some light reflects off the surface while other beams penetrate through and reflect from deeper down. These two light sources then interfere to make the shimmering patterns.

Wing structure

A bee wing under a microscope shows that it is made from an upper and lower surface of chitin – the same stuff as in the rest of the exoskeleton. The wing is then stiffened by an inner layer of haemolymph, which is the insect equivalent of blood, which carries oxygen and nutrients around the body. Instead of pumping through blood vessels, this colourless liquid washes through the body cavity.

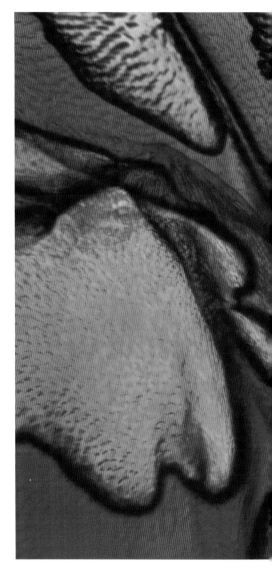

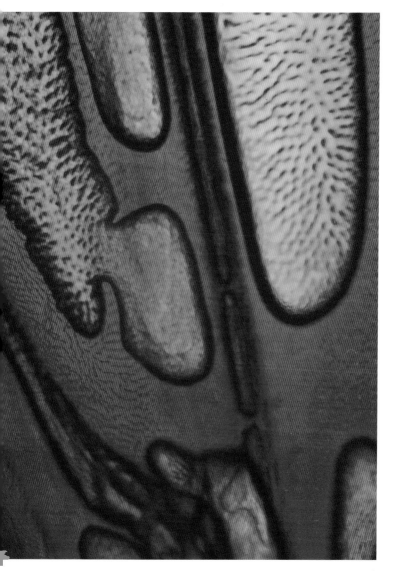

ABOVE:

Male sense

Despite being misnamed as a feeler, the antenna is an array of sophisticated sensory systems that detects chemicals and picks up vibrations. This male long-horned bee has longer antennae than the females because it is maximizing its ability to pick up the odours of potential mates.

OPPOSITE TOP:

Hearing

The bee's antenna has fine hairs that are linked to nerve cells. As these hairs waft in the currents of air that pass by, they are able to send motion information to the brain and also something like hearing signals, as loud noises create pressure waves in the air. Bees do not have true ears.

OPPOSITE BOTTOM:

Touch

Bee antennae also work as feelers, with nerve-linked mechanoreceptors clustered near their tips responding to touch and pressure.

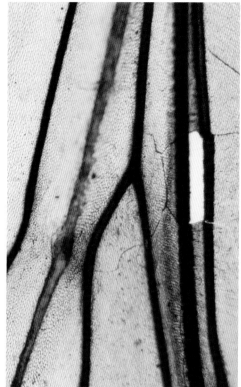

LEFT:

Motion sensors

The compound eye does not provide a detailed view of the surroundings. However, it is very good at picking up motion as an object moves across the eye.

ABOVE:

Vein support

The wing veins are a deeper and thicker region of the upper and lower cuticle that runs through the wing. This creates a rigid structure supporting the shape of the wing, with cross-branches adding more strength.

Clawed feet
A honeybee effortlessly grips to a smooth surface using its small but strong tarsal claws. There are three on each foot.

BELOW:
Cleaner
One unique feature of bee morphology is a brush-like structure on the front foreleg, which is used to clean the antennae and mouthparts.

RIGHT:
Grooved face
The bee's face is made up of two plates. The clypeus is like a lid sitting over the mouthparts, while the frons above it is more like a forehead. There is a distinct articulated groove.

Abdomen

There are few body parts as distinctive as a honeybee's abdomen. The yellow bands on a black background are an example of aposematism, where the animal is sending out a signal that attackers may come to harm. It probably evolved through the process of Mullerian mimicry where many species adopted the same signal and thus all species benefit from the other unrelated species spreading the message widely on their behalf.

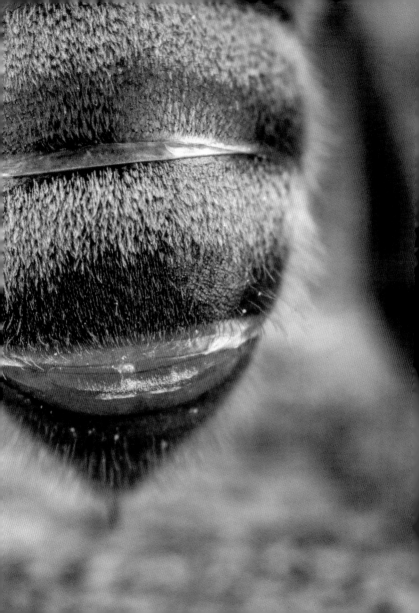

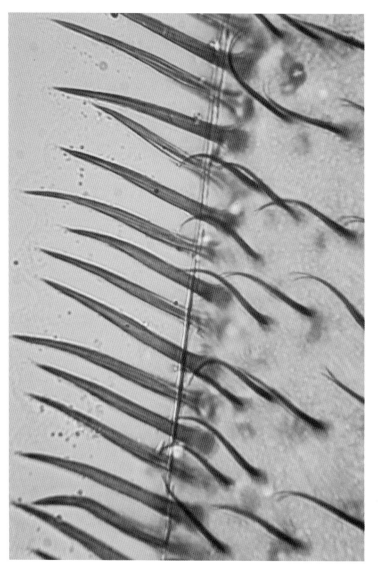

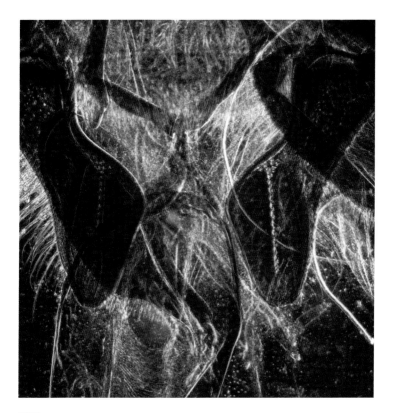

LEFT:

Waterproofing

Viewed up close, tiny hairs can be seen on a bee's wings. Quite what these hairs are for is unknown. It is possible that they work in a waterproofing capacity or they may be motion and air-flow sensors.

ABOVE:

Mandibles

This micrograph, or photograph taken with a microscope, shows the pincers of the two mandibles around the top of the mouth.

RIGHT:

Perfect pollinators in peril

The bee is a pollen- and nectar-collection machine that evolved about 100 million years ago – around the same time that flowering plants first appeared. Today, the world's bees are weighed down by the unwitting impact of human behaviours that destroy the bees' habitats and poison them with pollution.

OPPOSITE:

Simple eyes

All bees have three simple eyes, or ocelli, on the top of the head behind the antenna. These organs pick up changes in light level.

In the Hive

As the popular phrase says, a hive is always a place full of activity. How could it not be when there are hundreds, probably thousands, of individual bees all working toward the same goal. Among the seeming chaos, there is complete order. The queen controls every aspect of her workers' lives using a cocktail of chemical signals. These suppress the development of the workers' sexual organs, rendering them incapable of producing viable young. If the queen dies, workers rush to divert the development of a few larvae from worker to new queen. If they fail, then the colony is doomed. Some workers can lay eggs, but in almost all species of social bee, these eggs will only develop into male drones, who do not contribute to the running of the hive. The team works hard to prevent this disaster, and the queen is seldom exposed to danger.

And that same teamwork sees the hive through the very hardest of times, conditions that would not be survivable for insects living alone. The workers are able to refine a high-calorie food – namely honey – from the sparsest of ingredients: a weak sugar water and pollen dust. Most solitary bees will die off before the winter arrives, leaving only eggs behind. However, the honey diet sustains the colony through the winter, when other food sources are too scarce for such a number of insects. And when the good times roll, the hive will grow so large that the queen's chemical control begins to wane. When this happens, the bees prepare for a swarm. Watch out.

OPPOSITE:
Having a ball
A swarm of dwarf honeybees gathers in a ball of bodies on a lime tree. The queen is protected deep inside, as the colony searches for a place to construct a new hive.

Queen control

The queen bee wields
a chemical control
over her workers. The
pheromone production
goes hand in hand with
the queen's fertility.
Her hugely enlarged
ovaries make her
considerably larger than
her infertile workers.

OVERLEAF:

Broodcomb

The open brood cells
contain the chubby
grub-like larvae that are
growing inside. These
young bees are about
nine days old and will
soon have their cells
capped – as has already
happened next door.
Then they will pupate
for two weeks and
metamorphose into
an adult worker.

Pupation

Row upon row of pupae are lined up within the broodcomb. Inside the pupal skin, or cocoon, the insect has become dormant as its body is undergoing a wholesale transformation.

Rare beast

The queen uses a store of sperm collected from several males on her nuptial flight to fertilize most of the eggs she lays. These will be females, mostly workers of course, but a few new queens are produced from time to time. Some eggs are not fertilized and develop into male drones, which are larger than workers with obviously bigger eyes.

OPPOSITE:
Exploitation

Many animals are fond of eating honey. Perhaps the most famous are the bears and honey badgers, the latter of which is sometimes led to the nest by the honeyguide bird. Humans have also been recruited by the honeyguide for the same purpose in the past, but for the last few thousand years, we have gone one better and kept our honeybee colonies in hives that we control, using an intimate knowledge of bee behaviours.

PREVIOUS PAGES:
Swarm
Bees swarm over an apple tree. A colony of bees is
a superorganism, or a collection of organisms that
works as one living thing.

ABOVE:
Foragers
A white-tailed bumblebee collects food for the colony.
The forager caste of social bees tend to be the older
ones, who are unable to tend to larvae effectively.
Bumblebee foragers are among the fastest insects
around. They fly at speeds of 54km/h (33mph).

RIGHT:
Liquid fuel
Honeybees become foragers at the age of about
three weeks. They slurp up nectar from the nectarine
reservoirs at the base of a flower and store it in the
'honey stomach', a pouch at the top end of the gut.
Back at the hive, this nectar is regurgitated into
honeycomb cells.

Apiculture
A beekeeper inspects a frame, one of several that slots into a hive. The frame creates a space for the bees to build a wax honeycomb, but can also be removed easily to harvest the honey without damaging the wax matrix so workers can clean it up and start to fill the cells with honey again.

ABOVE:
Forest home
Honeybees are thought to have evolved in semi-desert habitats with extreme water restrictions and widely dispersed sources of low-quality foods. It is this ecology that gave rise to eusociality in other unrelated animals, such as termites and mole rats. However, the honeybee life plan has proven extremely adaptable, and hives can survive just about anywhere from forests to meadows, from the edge of the tundra to the desert.

RIGHT:
Queen cups
An apiarist tends to plastic queen cups containing queen bees' larvae, which are used to found new hives. In the wild, nurse bees supply these larvae with frequent doses of royal jelly, which drive their development into fully fertile females.

New home needed

These dwarf bees have just set out on their swarming adventure. Tropical bees, such as these, will swarm more often, because they are more likely to be driven to divide the colony due to high temperatures inside or a lack of water for all those workers.

Comings and goings
Forager bees must collectively fly a total of 86,000km (53,000 miles) to produce just 500g (1.1lb) of honey. This is a combined flight equivalent to 2.2 times around the world.

ABOVE:

The drone

A nurse bee is dwarfed by her drone brother. He will leave the colony with his fellow brothers and a virgin queen sister. They will scatter to avoid breeding among themselves. The drone will get one chance to breed, while the queen will have several mates before returning to the colony to take over the egg-production responsibilities.

RIGHT:

Pollen baskets

A honeybee forager has loaded up on pollen from an orange dahlia. The pollen is packed for the flight home in 'baskets' on the hind legs. These are a flattened area of the femur or 'thigh' with hooked protrusions that hold a mass of the sticky grains. The pollen basket is one possible derivation of the idiom 'bees' knees', as they represent the most important and refined part of the bee.

LEFT:
Food restrictions
This hive has been designed so returning forager bees can just squeeze through holes but most of the pollen is stripped from their legs in the process.

ABOVE:
Pollen trap
Supplies of pollen collected from bees build up in a pollen trap. Beekeepers will use this supply for feeding to hives early in the spring to kick-start honey production when flowers are still scarce.

Out with the old

A honeybee swarm is normally led by the older queen. She leaves a new generation of queens developing in her old nest, and recruits half the workers under her banner to fly off and set up a new nest somewhere else.

Communal living
Solitary mason bees often live communally, especially where a kindly person has set up an ideal habitat for their mud-lined nests. Despite being crowded together, all these bees are devoting their energies to ensuring the survival of their own young, not those of another.

ABOVE:
Meeting the cousins
An orchid bee feeds on a verbena watched by a worker ant (top) – tiny by comparison. The ant lives in a eusocial system just like a honeybee (but not an orchid bee) and, despite lacking wings, is a close relative of the bees.

RIGHT:
Nectar pump
The bees tongue, or glossa, is sheathed in a pair of maxillae, creating a near tube. The glossa flits up and down inside this tube to lift nectar up to the mouth.

OVERLEAF:
Search area
Bees flying into the hive deserve a good rest – but seldom get it. The foragers will search for food as far as 6km (3.6 miles) from the hive. Any further than that and the workers expend more energy bringing in the food than is available in the pollen and nectar.

Mud hives
Old-style mud beehives seen here in Germany work perfectly well but have to be destroyed to access the honey made inside.

Honey production

Nectar and pollen collected by the foragers is received on the honeycomb and stored in cells. The nectar dosed with a little pollen and wax is then reduced into a syrupy honey. This is achieved by workers fanning the liquid with their wings, driving off the water so it steadily thickens into a substance that is so sweet that it is relatively impervious to decay, just like fruit preserves and jams.

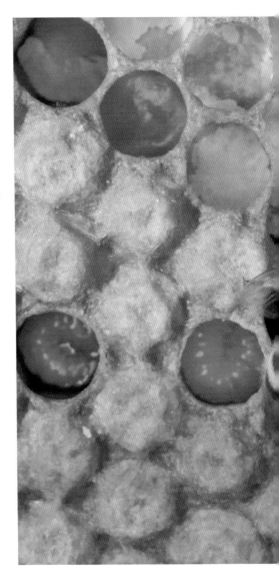

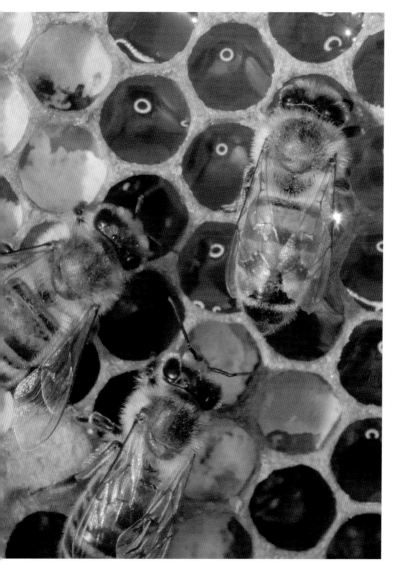

LEFT:
Bearding
A bee swarm will frequently 'beard' before setting off. This behaviour sees the bees gather near to the old nest, forming a distinct group that then sets off on its mission to find new lodgings.

ABOVE:
Nuisance call
Bees will set up home in any suitable cavity, be it in a hollow tree branch or artificial structure. A nest near to where people live needs to be removed because constant conflict between the two home owners is inevitable.

OPPOSITE TOP:
Queen cup
The brood cell of a
queen sits perpendicular
to the cells of the
workers. Once a colony
grows so large that
the queen's chemical
influence loses its power,
she will produce some
new queens, and prepare
to leave the nest for a
daughter to inherit.

OPPOSITE BOTTOM:
Future rivals
Three queen pupae are
close to splitting open so
the adult bee can emerge.
The first one out will
seek out her rival sisters
and sting them to death
within their cocoon.

LEFT:
New leader
The occupant of the
queen cup has been fed
royal jelly, which takes
a few more days than a
worker. This requires
a specialist team of
nurse bees. Nurse bees
can only produce royal
jelly for nine days before
their glands atrophy.
Once the queen has
emerged she is cleaned
and fed by attendants.

PREVIOUS PAGES:
Insect hotel
This collection of hollows, nooks and crevices has been provided as a home for bees and other insects. An insect house – or a hotel on this grand scale – provides the foundation for a healthy population of insects in a habitat.

ABOVE:
Wide choice
Honeybees are not beholden to any flower species in particular and are able to gather food from all shapes and sizes of bloom. The bees of some hives even collect the honeydew in place of nectar. This is a sweet liquid excreted from the anuses of sap-sucking aphids.

OPPOSITE:
Sea holly
Bumblebees, such as the white-tailed species *Bombus lucorum*, have a close association with sea holly and other members of the wild carrot family. These plants often have dense clusters of small flowers that create a one-stop shop for all the bee's needs.

Africanized bee

The Africanized honeybee is a artificial hybridization of African and European subspecies of *Apis mellifera*. This was carried out in 1956 in Brazil but several swarms of the new breed escaped into the wild. There is no significant physical difference between natural subspecies and this new strain, which has since spread across warmer areas of South and Central America and into the southwest of the United States.

RIGHT:

Danger?

The Africanized bee is sometimes called the killer bee. Between 500 and 1,000 bee stings in a short period carries a serious risk of death, and indeed people have been killed by Africanized bees. However, this is not because their stings are deadlier, but because they are more likely to attack a person nearing their nest.

Construction site
Wild worker honeybees are building a new home on a tree branch using yellow orange beeswax. The beeswax is secreted from glands in the abdomen. Wax workers are generally nurse bees that are too old to produce royal jelly anymore.

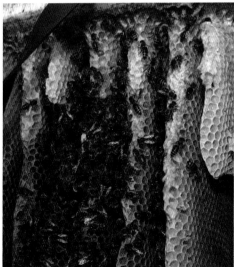

OPPOSITE:
Water cooler
It can be hot inside a hive, so hot it kills the brood. As the heat rises, some workers will leave the nest to make more room for cooling breezes, and other will increase airflow by fanning their wings. Foragers switch from nectar to water and slurp up a bellyful to squirt on to the honeycomb back at the hive.

LEFT TOP:
Cutting losses
A new bee nest has been abandoned after construction, with the comb cells largely empty. A queen will abscond like this when there is a lack of food sources nearby. A laying queen is too heavy to fly far, so she stops being fed, loses weight and shuts down her egg production, ready for the journey ahead.

LEFT BOTTOM:
Wild living
A wild honeybee nest will have several combs of cells with gallery space in between, a platform for the workers.

Beeswax

Workers busy themselves building cells. Each bee has eight wax glands, and these secrete a clear, colourless wax, which is a mixture of fatty acids and complex alcohols. They chew this into a more workable pulp and the yellow colour comes from the pollen grains that infect the workers and the nest.

Wasp attack

A bumblebee has met its match and is under attack from a parasitic wasp. The wasp looks like it has an immense sting but really that is an ovipositor, or tube for delivering an egg inside the body of the bee. The bee is paralysed by the attack and will become a zombie – still alive but immobile – which is slowly eaten from the inside by the wasp larvae that hatches inside.

Fire?

A beekeeper's smoke box signals to the bees that the area is on fire – they aren't to know that they live in a box. The approaching fire stimulates the bees to hurry inside and eat up as much honey as possible before it is destroyed. This imperative overrides any instinct to protect the nest and attack the invading human.

Protection

Beekeepers put themselves in harm's way to collect honey. Some have learned to be gentle enough not to invite attack from their captive bees, but most prefer to wear coveralls and a net face screen to minimize the stings.

ABOVE:

Ready-made home
The vertically hung
framed beehive design
dates from the mid-19th
century. The frame makes
it possible to reuse the
wax honeycomb. That
means that beekeepers
maximize honey yields
because a wax worker
bee must eat 8g (0.3oz)
of honey to produce 1g
(0.04oz) of beeswax.

RIGHT:

Winter feasting
Beekeepers must leave
some honey in the hive
for the colony to eat
during winter. It can get
so cold that the bees are
unable to move easily
from frame to frame, so
before the cold weather
hits, the keepers move all
the full frames together
to ensure the bees have
access to the food
they need.

LEFT:

Stingless beekeeping

A stingless beehive is very different to that of a honeybee. A covered tray sits atop a tree stump occupied by a stingless bee nest. The bees collect their honey in pots in the tray, which are then pumped out by the beekeeper.

ABOVE:

Honey hunter

A honey hunter in the forests of Cameroon wears traditional protective clothing while harvesting wild honey from a nest in a tree trunk.

Heave
A construction team of worker bees repairs a damaged comb with an active brood. To haul the damaged structure together, the bees must 'festoon' forming, a living sheet of bodies linked together by their tarsal claws.

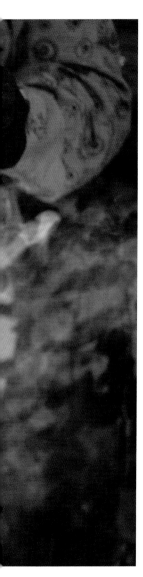

Harvest time
The smoke box subdues
the bees as the frame is
prepared for the honey to
be removed.

Uncapping
A beekeeper scrapes away
the wax caps that close
off the honeycomb so the
honey can flow out.

Honey press

A simple technique for extracting the honey is crush and strain, where the whole comb is mashed up and the honey filtered out from the mixture. Here honey extracted by a spinner is sieved to filter out fragments of wax.

Spin system

A less destructive method of collecting honey is to use a spinning extractor machine. Centrifugal force pushes the honey outward from the cells as the frames are spun. This oozing honey then trickles into the base for collection.

Ancient system
Ethiopian beekeepers living near Lake Chamo have hung traditionally-built hives made from long woven baskets from an acacia tree.

Bees and Flowers

Bees form the Anthophila grouping within the wider insect order, and that name means 'flower lover'. This is a testament to how these little insects are all specialist flower feeders, visiting to feast on the nectar and pollen provided by the blooms. Many species have adapted to exploit certain kinds of plant, even going as far as collecting the oils to anoint themselves with an alluring scent. In much the same way, plants have evolved to exploit their visitors, and today thousands of species rely on bees to pollinate them, including about a third of the commercial crops grown around the world – everything from onions and potatoes to coconuts and cashews. An insect-pollinated flower produces nectar purely to lure in bees and other creatures. It serves no other purpose. The pollen is especially sticky, unlike the grains of a wind-pollinated plant, which are microscopic to aid their dispersal. The plants must tolerate the majority of their pollen being taken away by bees as food. But a few grains will make it onto the legs and body of the roving insect caller, and cling there on the journey to the next flower or the next after that, where it is brushed on to the stigma of the flower, a sticky spatula for collecting incoming pollen. Assuming the pollen is from the right plant, it will begin a journey tunnelling into the heart of the flower to fertilize the plant's ovules or eggs. This is the first step in creating seeds and fruits that will transform into next year's blooms.

OPPOSITE:
For the bees
A dwarf honeybee, *Apis florea*, collects
nectar in a tropical bloom
in Southeast Asia.

Hover and lick
An orchid bee, *Euglossa intersecta*, hovers near a flower in the Amazon basin using its impressively long tongue, which is far longer than the mouthparts of other bees.

Waggle dance

A honeybee forager uses a waggle dance performed on the honeycomb to communicate the direction and distance from the hive to a good source of food. The direction is defined by the angle of the dance relative to the sun, and the number of waggles shows how far to fly. The surrounding bees pick up the information and set off to the food site.

Landing zone
This daisy offers a wide
and stable landing area
for the bees – more than
one at a time – to gather
food for the colony.

LEFT:
Slurping nectar
This orchid bee, *Euglossa imperialis*, is slurping up nectar from a tube-shaped flower in Costa Rica.

ABOVE:
Bee's-eye view
This tulip flower coated in water drops shows, under ultraviolet light, more of what a bee sees as it searches for food. The pollen and nectar-rich parts of the flower stand out against the petals.

Easy life

A cuckoo bee enjoys an easy life as it feeds on a coral vine. It need only feed itself, slurping up the choicest nectars and nibbling on the best pollens, unencumbered by the need to collect food for its young. Another bee species is doing that job for it!

ABOVE:

Resource management

A squad of foragers from a honeybee hive work together to strip the food resources from a head of blooms. If they do not, then a neighbouring colony will have it all for sure.

RIGHT:

Honey stomach

A western honeybee is ingesting this flower's nectar. It puts the liquid in the proventriculus, a pouch just above the stomach. In here the nectar is not digested very rapidly, and is then regurgitated into cells.

LEFT:

Happy accident

A honeybee has a face full of pollen after making the most of a yellow flower. The transfer of pollen from flower to flower is left to chance, but if the flower attracts enough visitors the odds are narrowed.

ABOVE:

Fully laden

A bee hovering near a pussy willow blossom has a good supply of pollen in its baskets. These tough foragers can carry up to 80 percent of their body weight in pollen.

Hanging food
Bees are highly adaptable
and can make use of
all kinds of flowers.
Here they use their
claws to cling to flimsy
inflorescences.

Orchid partnership
A metallic orchid bee searches for nectar in an orchid. Only these bees visit these esoteric blooms, which will not pollinate without their shiny green partner.

Haulage
Once a forager, always a forager. The magnified image shows that honeybees are covered in specks of pollen that are an inevitable result of its job. Foraging is the last role of a worker. Most die at the age of seven weeks.

LEFT:
Brush past

A red hibiscus has cleverly evolved so the hefty bumblebee cannot get to the nectar without rubbing up against the flower's anthers, or pollen holders.

ABOVE:
Digging deep

A honeybee wriggles up inside a tubular flower, being dusted with pollen – and passing on grains from the last flower – as it goes.

OVERLEAF:
Sticky dust

A honeybee is covered in pollen from a sunflower. There is little doubt it will pass at least some to a neighbouring flower.

Picture Credits